THE

COLOR

OF PAIN

THE
COLOR
OF PAIN

BOYS WHO ARE SEXUALLY ABUSED
AND THE MEN THEY BECOME

GREGORY REID

LIGHTHOUSE TRAILS PUBLISHING
EUREKA, MONTANA

THE COLOR OF PAIN
© 2010 Gregory Reid
First Edition

Published by
Lighthouse Trails Publishing
P.O. Box 908
Eureka, MT 59917
(see back of book for publisher and author contact information)

Library of Congress Cataloging-in-Publication Data

Reid, Gregory, 1954-
   The color of pain : boys who are sexually abused and the men they become / Gregory Reid. ~ 1st ed.
      p. cm.
   ISBN 978-0-9824881-7-1 (softbound : alk. paper)
   1. Sexually abused boys. 2. Male sexual abuse victims. 3. Adult child sexual abuse victims. I. Title.
   HV6570.R44 2010
   362.76~dc22
                                        2010038559

Note: Lighthouse Trails Publishing books are available at special quantity discounts. Contact information for publisher in back of book.

Printed in the United States of America

DEDICATION

For Joel, Johnny, Jacob, Joshua, Bryan, and all the brave little guys whose time to heal is coming.

For Mark . . . this book is really for you.

* * * * *

Publisher's Note: The photographs on both the cover and throughout this book are taken from stock photos and used for illustrative purposes only. It is not to be implied that any of these persons are the victims of abuse.

Caution: This book deals with sensitive issues; it should not be read or reviewed by young children. Parents and teachers should use discernment and wisdom to determine the appropriate age for their children or students to read it.

* * * * *

acknowledgments

I want to thank those who have encouraged me by their work on behalf of abused kids and victims: Nadine McIntosh, Ester Flores, Beth Stokes, Reta Johnston,

. . . and my heartfelt love and prayers to the brave parents, grandparents, and relatives, who know full well why this book needed to be written: Lori, JoAnne, JoEllen, Jacque, Norman, Greg, Diane, Nola, and all the Believe the Children parents,

. . . and the special friends who gave me courage and time and support: Erin, Ben Kennedy, Susan & Bryant, and especially my best friend who was with me as I grieved my mother's death and had the audacity and right insight to suggest I needed to do this book. Your timing was perfect. Thanks.

. . . a special thank you to Lauren, who though now passed from this world and who suffered so much while here, remains a true encouragement and inspiration to me because of her bravery for telling the truth, even when many did not believe her,

. . . and final thanks to Captain Chris Bratton, a mentor in my work fighting child abuse, who by his time and encouragement helped me to believe I had a valuable contribution to make to boys and men who had been molested. God bless you Chris.

CONTENTS

Preface

AS a youth minister and someone who has worked in the law enforcement field advocating for kids who have been sexually abused, I saw a great need for a book that was specifically written for those who have been abused as boys. I found there was very little written about that difficult subject, and much of what was available was unhelpful, if not completely useless.

I realized that probably no one was more qualified to write such a book as someone who had suffered such abuse and grown up and healed. I realized I could be that person.

I began writing, not knowing how long it would take or how hard it might be. To my surprise, I was able to complete the first draft within a month. I first self-published this book under the title *Orphans in the Storm*—I am grateful that first edition was distributed fairly widely and hopefully helped a lot of kids who were afraid to talk—afraid someone would find out their terrible secret. After all, no one likes to admit that boys get abused too. That is why I was in my thirties before I told anyone my worst secrets.

Part one of this book is more for professionals, pastors, and concerned family and friends. More stats and facts. The more people that know those things, the less chance others will be victims of pedophile predators.

Part two was written from my heart—for survivors, from a survivor. It is not slick or polished—just me bleeding on paper and spilling my guts. I hope it helps others to know they are not alone in their suffering and isolation—and to know they too can find healing and dignity again.

GREGORY REID

Have mercy upon me, O Lord, for I am in trouble: mine eye is consumed with grief, yea, my soul and my belly. For my life is spent with grief, and my years with sighing. Psalm 31: 9-10

INTRODUCTION

I'M a male sexual-abuse survivor. I'm also a ritual-abuse survivor.[1] I am rare, and belong to a company of men and boys, mostly silent and scared. So few have survived well enough to talk about it. I know I have to talk, because I DID survive, and because I see them in every group I meet, from five to seventy-years-old suffering, silent victims who are not really considered REAL victims by many, since the male species, in their minds, should be able to fend off any abuse. No matter how little they were. No matter how bad and scary it was. So we keep mostly quiet, to avoid the humiliation of questioning, cynical eyes that seem to say, "Come on, you could have done SOMETHING to stop it!" Can you imagine the public outrage in most places nowadays if you said that to a female rape victim? But no one really defends boy and men victims. So we've stayed silent. Wouldn't you? If you're a victim, you probably do. You probably picked this book up with a big knot of fear in your gut, hoping no one would suspect you might be one of the one in six boys who are sexually abused.

I want to tell you, you've got nothing to be afraid of. After all, being molested was something that was done *to* you, and you shouldn't feel you have to apologize for looking for some hope, that you feel you have to hide because of someone else's sins against you. Do those who are cynical have any idea what it's like, what it feels like, how much pain it causes? Then forget about the doubters. You need a friend, and I hope you just picked it up—a book with a voice, one you'll know is also maybe yours and one that is warm and real. A voice, mainly, of a brother who's struggling out of his pain, too.

I try not to look too hard at how much progress I've made; I get too introspective, and then it goes into self-pity, and that's worse than anything I can think of. When things about being molested come up, I do my best to face it. I've totally overcome some things (like blaming myself) but I'm still struggling with others (like being afraid that it's written all over my forehead and people just "know"). Some struggles are no surprise, some are very fresh and event sensitive, and some knock me sideways when I'm not expecting any more to handle. But now I have hope, because little by little I've been healed, and I want to give a little of that to you.

I've written from my history, my head, and my heart. There's not a lot of statistics, but I've put in a few for those who just want to help. A lot of the following is from my own experience, as graphic and real as I dare. For me, no one knew. No one should have to struggle that way. Accept this as a gift from a friend to let you know YOU'RE NOT ALONE.

Part One

Just The Facts

First, My Own Story

In my autobiography, *Nobody's Angel*, I tell the story of my life, and how the first eleven years of my childhood were a black hole of emptiness. Things had happened, but they had been so horrific I had entered into a world of Forget. I went from a once polite, gentle, God-loving child, changed overnight into a slovenly, sexualized, angry, hard-drinking, rebellious, destructive, secretive, occult-addicted pre-adolescent. My father asked me once, "Whatever happened to that neat little boy I used to know?"

"He died a long time ago, Pop," I replied, though I knew he couldn't understand.

Starting at eleven-years-old, I entered the world of the occult. I was drawn into the darkness of it and never could grasp why. I was exploited by predators, raped, and abused and experienced all types of evil. This went on until I felt that I was at the brink of death. A staggering sense of loss and grief had become my constant companions. By the time I was fifteen, I had lived what felt like an entire pathetic life.

I guess my parents should have asked more questions about the changes in me, but at the time they were struggling with serious health issues, and their lives couldn't take on anymore than what was already consuming them.

In the spring of my 15th year, I met a man hitchhiking who turned out to be a Christian. He gave me a copy of a book called *The Cross and The Switchblade*. It was the story of Dave Wilkerson, a skinny Pennsylvania preacher, who went to New York and faced down the worst, most deadly gang leader in New York, Nicky Cruz, and told him Jesus loved him. Nicky beat him up. Dave kept on him, and Nicky finally became a Christian.

Eventually, after some very dramatic events, I too surrendered my life to Jesus Christ and became a Christian. Had that not happened, I believe I would have died before ever reaching the age of twenty. I had been on a road to destruction.

Over the next few years, I continued to heal under the protection of some dear Christian friends and a seventy-six-year-old Baptist saint who took me in and loved me and taught me about God's unconditional love. I devoured the Scriptures, and they broke the lies. I fought a vicious battle with sexual issues, depression, unhealthy relationships, deep loneliness, and a smoldering rage.

I went immediately into "ministry" at sixteen, and before I was twenty-six, had been around the world. The occult, and demonic influence, had wrapped itself in every fiber of my being, and God gently and firmly took me out of it all.

How was I to know that everything inside me would fall apart in my twenties, when as a respected teacher and youth leader, I would have to face a nightmare worse than anything I could imagine? God was now ready for the ordeal to come to me that I know broke His heart, but would be the final deliverance and revelation of who I was and where I had been. I was about to go to the gates of hell—not as a warrior—but as a wanted man, a traitor to the devil, and a terrified child. Those first forgotten eleven years of my life were about to intrude into my adult existence. I had to go back into the dark and empty corridors of my forgotten past to retrieve the truth and, in so doing, become fully prepared to go to war against the satanic powers, organizations, and occult rulers who continue to destroy the lives of thousands of innocent children today.

It was the summer of my twentieth year, and I was home from Bible school for three months. It was the beginning of the crack in the wall that would lead to my descent into the mouth of my satanic past. Nearly a decade would pass before all of the horrible ugly truth came out. But the Lord was with me all along the way; and today I can say that He has healed me. Yes, there are and always will be scars, but His love and His Word have been my Deliverer.

There are those who say that people who forget some part of their pasts are delusional and psychotic when they suddenly or even gradually remember. One such organization, the False Memory Syndrome Association, has devoted itself to "proving" that such remembrances are never true or at least very rarely. I would be one of those whom they would call delusional.

I've watched for years as this organization has grown, wreaking havoc every place they go. They have crushed victims and sent little children back into abusive homes.

They claim recovered memory victims are mostly hysterical females with a history of mental illness whose memories were implanted by clever therapists. I know there are times that does indeed happen. The abuse bandwagon has had some bad baggage, bitter people seeking vengeance, custody disputes, and New Age mystical craziness.

But they are wrong as wrong can be to lump together all those saying they remember a forgotten past of being abused. I'm a male, non hysterical, with no history of mental illness or hospitalization, and my memories were worked through solo—no therapist. In other words, I don't fit their degrading, neat little profile. I can't be accused of "survivor network sharing" suggestibility or "Munchausen Syndrome"[1] because my memories were found before I even met another survivor.

When a child or pre-adolescent has been sexually abused, it creates an intolerable situation for the child. Their young cognitive minds simply cannot handle it. When they are going through the abuse, in order to survive it, they must mentally separate from it—it would be like putting it into a suitcase, stuffing it out of the way. As they enter their teen years, they are carrying on their back, so to speak, this suitcase that now weighs a ton. That is why so many teens who were abused as children turn into extremely troubled teens, especially for those who have never been able to tell their secret or who have managed to forget it all together. Later, somewhere in their adult lives, that weight cannot be carried any longer, and it begins to come out—they start to remember what had been forgotten. At that point of their lives, how those around them respond is of utmost importance. Will they be believed? Will they be ridiculed or now looked upon as weird, perverts, or gay? In *The Color of Pain*, I hope to help not only those boys and men who were abused but also help their families and trusted friends so that healing and restoration can finally take place.

LOOKING FOR THE SIGNS

THIS is for those with children and teens, and those who work with them. It's also for abuse survivors still not convinced that they were abused. Having one or two of these may be normal or not a sign of abuse, but the more that apply, the more likely abuse has happened.

Lack of Feelings _____

Rage _____

Substance Abuse _____

Promiscuity _____

Secrecy _____

Withdrawal _____

Aversion to Touch _____

Distrust _____

Genital Rashes _____

Exhibitionism _____

Dissociation _____

Stomach Pains _____

Lethargy _____

Frequent Illness _____

Trance Outs _____
Terror Nightmares _____
Fear of Adults ____
Crying Jags _____
Self-Mutilation _____
Attention Deficit _____
Sensual Dress/Posture_____
Extreme Privacy Need _____
Extreme Control Need _____
Excessive Masturbation _____
Age Inappropriate Sexual Knowledge _____
Extreme, unreasonable fears _____
Extreme Need for Order _____
Fear of Public Rest rooms _____
Clinging to Adults _____
Fear of Abandonment _____
Rebellion Against Authority _____
Excessive Modesty _____
Intestinal Problems _____
Flashbacks _____
Body Memories _____
Rage Toward Parents, especially father _____

WHERE PREDATORS HUNT

PREDATORS looking for boys and teens to molest want to be in situations of access or trust to the target kids. These are some of the most likely places predators find that access:

Schools as teachers, coaches, librarians, custodians, etc.

Boy Scout groups, Big Brother programs

Churches & youth groups

Libraries, bookstores, adult bookstores

Public parks

Health spas, YMCAs

Motels & hotels

Malls, movie theaters

Picking up hitchhikers

Beaches & lakes

Video arcades,
Miniature golf courses

Dungeons & Dragons
& Other fantasy
related setups

Bowling alleys &
skating rinks

Daycare centers

Internet chat rooms,
news groups, kids'
websites and forums

Myths about Abused Boys

Myth: It is not a widespread problem.
Fact: One in every ten men & boys, and some say one in six has possibly been molested in some form.

Myth: Most molesters are dirty old men.
Fact: Most predators are highly intelligent career people with community respect and a good income.

Myth: Most predators are stranger to the child.
Fact: Stranger molestation is the exception, and most boys know their molesters well, as relatives for whom trust comes naturally or family friends or people in authority who have pursued the child to seduce them over a long period of time.

Myth: Abuse must be forced or violent to be called rape.
Fact: Any time an adult lures a child to sexual acts it's rape.

Myth: If the abuse was pleasurable for the boy, it was not rape.
Fact: Sex is a biological stimulus. Feeling pleasure may be a natural, but it is still a crime that a powerful, older person took an underage child or teen and used them for their own

gratification and the psychological and emotional damage done to the child is still just as real.

Myth: Most victims become abusers.
Fact: This is largely a jailhouse excuse for predators. Some do go on to abuse: some become violent but most just live self-destructive, miserable lives until they get help. But the fact is most boys who were molested do *not* grow up to molest. Furthermore, when a victim of abuse commits himself to the Lord and God's Word as a born-again Christian, an avenue for true healing is opened.

Myth: Non forced abuse makes the boy responsible.
Fact: No child is ever responsible for being raped.

Myth: It happens to other people's kids.
Fact: Molestation of boys is one of the most unreported crimes that exists. It COULD be your child. Communication, unconditional love, and acceptance is the only way to keep the door open to your son if something does or did happen.

Types of abuse and abusers

1. Stranger/forced/violent (rare)

2. Seduction (most common)

3. Strictly sex (less common)

4. "Relationship" abuse. This is where the predator exerts a great deal of time, energy, money and attention on his victim to prep them for sex. The molester has an ongoing interest in a fantasy/romantic relationship with the child/teen until, of course, they grow up, when they are discarded.

5. Incest (fairly common)

6. Pornographic abuse.
Both the use of pornography as a lure and the taking of photographs and videos of sex with the boy or teen is a fairly common practice with predators.

7. Prostitution abuse.
Paying for sex with a boy on the streets or elsewhere is still rape.

8. Voyeur abuse.
Seeking out a boy or boys to view them naked is abuse.

9. Exhibitionistic abuse.
An adult who exposes himself deliberately to a boy or teen for his own sexual gratification is abusing him.

10. Emotional abuse.
The worst damage inflicted by sexual predators on their victims is emotional manipulation, control, broken trust, threats, confusion, etc.

WHAT A VICTIM LOOKS LIKE

BOYS who get molested hide well, and it's not always easy to tell who they are. But there are certain things that make a potential victim vulnerable, and make them "desirable" to a predator.

1. Four- to sixteen-years-old.

2. "Innocent" appearance (to Predators this is very important)

3. Lonely, friendless, lost looking.

4. Starved for attention and affection.

5. Absent or emotionally distant father.

6. Sexually naive or inexperienced.

7. At a sexually awakened and experimental stage.

8. Emotionally pliable and easily trusting.

9. Identity unformed.

10. Looking for a hero.

11. Self-conscious about looks, insecure and shy.

What Not to Tell Us

WE may look tough on the outside or able to handle things well, but it's mainly a disguise. We're pretty fragile, and what you say to us when you discover where we've been could make the difference between us getting help or turning help away forever. That's especially true if we're little boys or teens. Every word you say counts. For all of us, here's some things you should never say when you find out what's happened to us:

1. How could you do that?

> It was done TO me. I had no choice!

2. Why didn't you stop it?

> We couldn't stop it. It was too unexpected, too powerful, they were bigger, we trusted them, and we had no way of knowing what would happen if we said no. How did we know they wouldn't kill us or tell everyone we made it happen?

3. Why didn't you kick them and run?

> We were paralyzed. The fear of what was happening
> was so strong that we had no choice except to let it
> happen. WE COULDN'T MOVE!

4. You should have told us!

> We were afraid to. We were afraid you'd hate us and
> blame us. They said you would.

5. Let's not talk about it.

> WE NEED TO TALK ABOUT IT! When you say
> that, you make us feel like we don't matter, our hurt
> doesn't matter, that you're just concerned about
> yourself and you don't care about anything but
> getting us to shut up.

6. What will people think of our family?

> Aren't we family? How do you think I feel about
> myself? If you're more concerned about our
> reputation than about me, then I'll just withdraw
> and not have a family anymore.

7. Didn't you know you were sinning?

> No, we didn't. And we weren't. You forget that this
> was done TO us, not something we asked for.

8. Let's not mention this again.

> Why not? You make us feel like nothing happened,
> that it wasn't any big deal, but it was, and we know
> it. If you won't talk to us or let us talk, we'll explode.

9. Forget about the past. You can't change it.

> But it's changed US. We can't forget. It's like you're telling a cancer patient to forget about his disease. If there's a cure (and there is for abuse) for God's sake don't keep it from us by denying where we've been.

10. How long is it going to take for you to get over this and get on with your life?

> I don't know. You tell ME. I bet you don't know, because you don't feel this devastating anger and hurt and sense of loss. It will take as long as it needs to, and we need you to accept us no matter how long it takes. Nobody wants to get through this more than we do.

A Predator's Toolkit

MOST "professional pedophiles" have turned molestation into a fine science. They are precise in their plans and use well tested lures and traps to get kids in a place where they can be molested. The following is a "profile of seduction," an overview of how a predator works.

LURES

1. Drugs (Voluntary and involuntary)

2. Alcohol (To lower the victim's inhibitions and make them confused and vulnerable)

3. Pornography (Printed and video, to lower the sexual inhibitions and arouse the victim)

4. Music, video games, etc.
The predator is current on music trends, video games, movies, etc. and their homes often look like a kid's paradise.

5. Prestige & Status.

To a boy or teen, hanging around with a dynamic, fun adult with a nice house and a fast car is a very powerful lure, a major ego booster.

6. Money & Gifts.
Predators shower their victims with gifts and money, which is very seductive to a kid who may not have much materially, and it also puts the boy in a place of "obligation" to the giver.

7. Physical affection.
Predators can sense kids who have little affection at home, which is something every boy or teen needs, and he slowly begins giving that affection to the boy a little at a time, making him dependent on it, craving it to feel loved and liked and special.

8. Emotional support.
Predators go out of their way to listen to a boy, sympathize with his problems and offer help and advice as well as encouragement. This goes a long way with a kid who doesn't feel like he's worth much.

9. Sexual gratification.
Predators are experts on how to seduce, entice, arouse and sexually stimulate a boy or teen, and like it or not, it can become an addiction for the boy, especially if it's his first sexual experience. Mix that with needed affection, and soon the boy won't know the difference between sex and affection, love and arousal.

10. Time.
Time is the predator's most powerful tool. Unlike normal adults who have lives, jobs, children, families, hobbies, and other interests and obligations which all play important but somewhat equal parts in life, the predator has a job, a career, interests, hobbies,

etc., only as props to support his addiction—kids. Since this is his all consuming addiction, money, time, and interests are all expended toward this one goal—to find his fantasy child or teen and molest them, photograph them, use them. Since the other things like work and family are just asides, they have enormous amounts of time and energy to devote to the finding of kids, the luring of kids, the prepping of kids, for the seemingly endless amount of time spent listening to kids and going places with them and buying them things and doing things with them, all in hopes of the ultimate—sex with a minor.

THE Project

Once a predator determines to find a victim, this is the general train of events that often follows:

1. He finds the desired child or teen.

2. Befriends them, gains their trust.

3. Gains the trust of the parents so they won't suspect.

4. Makes the boy feel important through lots of time and personal attention, makes him feel he is more important to him than anybody.

5. Flatters him. Tells him he's handsome, smart, etc.

6. Makes plans for private time with him,
   a. Counseling him,
   b. Going to movies,
   c. Going to the park, video arcade, beach, pool, concerts, etc.,
   d. Plans a camping trip with him,

e. Hires him to work around the house or business,
f. Helps him with his schoolwork.

7. Treats him like an adult.

8. Builds non threatening affectionate physical contact.

9. Introduces or allows "adult" activities; smoking, drinking, drugs, pornography, swearing, etc.

10. Starts slowly discussing sex, gaining as much intimate knowledge of him as possible.

11. Remolds his thinking about what is "normal sex," eventually disclosing his "normal" desires for sex with the boy.

12. Having changed his thinking, gained his trust and dependency and accelerated physical contact, the boy is now totally vulnerable to being molested.

13. The predator plans the time and place where there will be no suspicion or interference or time constraints.

14. After prepping him with alcohol, pornography, etc., while he has broken down the walls enough to start molesting him, he tells him:
It's normal.
All guys do it.
He knows some of his friends who do it.
He loves him.
The boy is "turned on" and that's normal and means he wants it too.
Guilt is wrong.
He's the greatest kid in the world.

15. After he's molested him, he makes the boy feel he started it, threatens to tell if he has to, tells him he will be destroyed if the boy tells—whatever it takes to keep him quiet.

16. After he has outgrown his attraction for him, the predator keeps the photos or videos as a memento and searches for a new kid.

This is a general picture that doesn't fit every victim or every predator, but fits many of them, and in that respect it is very painfully accurate. Knowing your enemy is half the battle in stopping him.

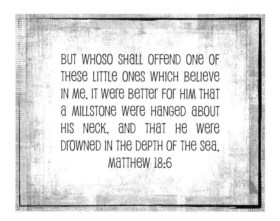

BUT WHOSO SHALL OFFEND ONE OF THESE LITTLE ONES WHICH BELIEVE IN ME, IT WERE BETTER FOR HIM THAT A MILLSTONE WERE HANGED ABOUT HIS NECK, AND THAT HE WERE DROWNED IN THE DEPTH OF THE SEA.
MATTHEW 18:6

Part Two

The Heart of the Matter

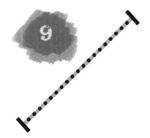

Sleeping . . . Sort of

A friend calls it "combat sleep." I call it hell. I never quite get there, suspended one blink away from awake at all times. Little creaks in the house, a car door, a sudden wind are all it takes to rip me out of sleep, heart pounding and all sweaty, left in the deep night to try desperately to succumb to sleep once again while my mind races wildly about nothing . . . over anything.

I am afraid to sleep. I'm afraid shadows will come while I am unable to wake, and I will be awakened, trapped, raped. Sleep is not safe for me.

And the dreams . . . suffocating, choking nightmares of death and pain and loneliness and longing and abandonment. Females who are predators. Men who are deadly, overpowering giants. Dreams of longing that wake me crying. Dreams of desire that leave me ashamed.

There is no escape, even in sleep. And so I remain the Vigilant Soldier over my tattered innocence.

The Hurt of Being Different

WE'RE not like you. We know it. Through no fault of our own, we've been permanently changed. We've become a separate breed, longing to be same as you, to feel like you, to be free of the shadow that covers our hearts. We are brave, and we hide well. Friendship is hard and trust even harder. We know we test, and withdraw, we probe and we defend ourselves. Because we're wary, and scared, and if you manage to hang around long enough and hang in there and give us time and don't run and earn our trust, you'll have a friend for life.

We're different because the sound of children laughing makes us sad, and close families make us think of what we lost. We try to be "one of the guys," but it's a lot of show because that part of us that used to not have to be on guard around our own kind was destroyed, so we never really let down the walls. Competition becomes a threat, and we play angry, to win—to prove we're strong. Or, we don't compete at all because to lose means we're powerless and helpless, and it's too scary to be there anymore.

We can't be spontaneous and childlike like you. We learn the scripts to make us seem like you, but we prefer total control over everything around us—our emotions, our possessions, our schedules. No surprises or being spooked from behind. So please don't get mad if we get angry because you're late and didn't call, or break a commitment, or change the radio station in our car without asking, because we're not going to let anyone take control again. It's not you. It's them.

We're different because our affection signals are all screwed up, and sometimes we'll ask you to back off and sometimes our eyes will plead to be held. There's no rule book to help you know when to do what, but please stay around long enough to figure it out.

We're cynical, and it means we've been betrayed; we're "cold," and it means we're scared and hurt. We don't respond to "what's wrong?" because we probably don't know, and we reject demands to "open up" because we will when we can, not on command.

It hurts to be different, but someday, maybe we'll grow enough to accept the scars and find real healing; and we'll always be different, but it won't hurt so bad anymore—because someone like you stayed with us and gave us patient love and accepted us no matter what. And maybe then we'll know being different isn't all that bad. Because maybe then we'll find another like us, and we'll help them to heal, too.

DOUBT AND DENIAL

THE hardest person to convince of some of my memories of abuse has been me. When some of them came, it was so frighteningly real, I shook for days afterward. But then, as most victims know, it receded and seemed . . . well, unreal. It took a long time to face the full truth.

Typical male, I needed proof. So I spent years validating what I was remembering. I learned a lot, returning to the "scene of the crimes," photographing houses, talking to experts, and finding my recall of objects, rituals, places, times, and people were not only accurate, but validated by other victims. You can imagine my shock when I met another survivor whose birthday and year of birth were the same as mine and whose ritual abuse took place at the same age in the same town!

Well, no, there's no "concrete evidence." Just physical scars and nightmares and flashbacks and crippling pain. But when I want to deny, I now have to get around some obstacles: Like, why is 90 percent of that time frame as a child totally blank? That's not normal. SOMETHING happened during that time. Since denying doesn't explain the lack of recall of those years OR the scars on my body, and since accepting my memories as real explains ALL the missing pieces that have plagued me for so many years, and since accepting the memories as real has brought healing and release (not deception and blame shifting), I've finally killed denial and become a survivor with an attitude. Don't tell ME I made it up!!!

My new stance came five years ago. I had just recalled one of my worst memories so far being used in child porn. I had lunch with a friend, one who knew what I was going through. At least I thought he did. His silence as I explained what I was working through betrayed him. He never said it, but he didn't believe me. And I needed him to! (Don't we all, at first?)

As I began to tell him about it over lunch, I felt the "little kid" inside me climb up the ladder to my eyes and peer out at my friend as I talked. Abruptly, suddenly, my friend said, "Don't you think you need to forget all this? The Bible says you're a new person in Christ and you need to forget what's behind." Suddenly, I felt that little kid scurry back down the ladder, slam the door shut and lock it on my friend for good. I would never be able to trust him with my past again. And I haven't. But with that experience, my inner need for approval, acceptance, and validation ended. I knew. I no longer needed others to believe an experience they hadn't walked through themselves?

My confidence has grown with the realization that something really happened to me. I believe, because I was there. I speak, because there are others. I persist, because I want to be free.

A note to my Christian family, the church that I love and belong to, whoever you are: "Forgetting what lies behind" is a process. Paul the Apostle didn't say, "Just forget about it, grow up and get on with your life." He often referred to his past, didn't he? Just because I have to go back to get me back and to let go doesn't mean I'm not going on. In fact, if I don't I'll never be free to go on. Paul also said, if you read Greek, that old things are PASSING away. All things are BECOMING new. It takes TIME. Please don't try to "quick fix" those of us who have lost so much. Just pray for us and be a friend.

Know that it is much harder for us to accept what we are remembering, what we've been through, than it is for you.

Sadness

I used to hate feeling sad. It meant something was really wrong with me. But I never quite knew what. So I turned it into other things, like anger, or too much T.V., or drinking binges, or isolation.

There's two words I came to hate hearing: "Cheer up!" Easy for you to say! Even well meaning and persistent friends saying, "What's wrong?" really annoys me. Like I know what's wrong! That's the problem. I usually don't. Sadness is a symptom, a slow nudge, a gentle tap on the shoulder that says, "Look at your heart. Something's hurting."

So instead of ignoring sadness or changing it or deadening it with various painkillers like booze or sex, I've learned to just go with it. Wherever it takes me. However long it needs to. Whatever the outcome.

I've made sadness one of my dearest and trusted friends. Trusted, because he is always leading me to the hurt and the healing. Dearest, because he lets me know my own heart is real and can still feel.

For those of us who were molested, seduced, and abused, sadness lets us feel our loss of innocence, of "normal," of sexual awakening, of family, of life.

It's the sadness of a little boy or a young teen who trusted an older friend or adult or father, or uncle, priest, teacher—and for that trust was rewarded with sick touch, and fondling, and pornography, and betrayal.

It is the sadness of one who needed affection and protection and to be held and to be led and to be sheltered and to be wanted and liked and, got some of that along with the price tag of allowing an adult to use our body for their own pleasure, or forced to do something sexual to an adult and so carry the guilt of it. "Well, you did it to me too, didn't you?"

It is the sadness of a kid who enters adolescence with a ton of guilt and fear, feeling responsible for being raped, feeling confused because he may still love the abuser, feeling afraid that the acts committed makes him "queer."

And the worst sadness is that he is still lonely, and needs to be held, and needs to be protected, and loved, and liked—but no one can be trusted anymore.

I'm thankful for sadness because he makes me know what I've lost so I can cry and grieve and

let it go. Almost anything can bring on sadness, but some things especially—a movie where a father figure defends or rescues a child or befriends a lonely teen boy, seeing warm loving fathers and mothers kissing and holding and playing with their little children, fathers playing baseball with their sons, summer mornings all lonely and quiet, and the sound of children playing without me somewhere . . .

And I embrace the sadness. I drink it in, and I weep, and I grieve for the child I was who had no touch or kiss, who had no friends, who lay paralyzed while others violated his trusting soul and stole his heart and locked him in jagged chains. I weep. And I sigh as healing tears dry, and I get back part of my tortured, innocent heart.

Please don't tell us to "cheer up" or ask why we don't just smile—as if that was a magical solution to wipe away years of anguish and lonely loss, and don't ask why we don't have the "Joy of the Lord." I NEED my sadness. The door to joy is found in embracing my sorrow and loss.

> THESE THINGS I HAVE SPOKEN UNTO YOU, THAT IN ME YE MIGHT HAVE PEACE. IN THE WORLD YE SHALL HAVE TRIBULATION: BUT BE OF GOOD CHEER; I HAVE OVERCOME THE WORLD.
> JOHN 16:33

Telling the Secret

THERE'S nothing more powerful than finding someone safe to tell "the secret" to. No one knows how hard it is, unless they've been there. Your heart pounds, your body is rock rigid, you grind your teeth, your mouth is dry. You think of all the excuses to keep your mouth shut. They'll get mad. They'll laugh. They'll reject you. They'll treat it like it was nothing and tell you to forget about it. Or worse: they'll be polite, nod their head like they understand, leave and not ever have anything to do with you again. But you have to tell someone, and oh God, please let it be the right one!

Finding someone to tell who's also been through it is the most incredible healing thing and the most rare.

Even then, the depth of doubt, self-hate, fear and insecurity is so strong, that even if you should tell someone who's been through it too, you leave and wonder, did I say too much? Did I do the right thing? Will they hate me? Only experience lets you know your trust wasn't for nothing.

Just getting to the point of telling fills you with mental and emotional mine fields. All the buried messages we learned to keep us quiet suddenly come to mind, some placed in us by the ones who molested us.

If you tell, I'll kill you.
If you tell, I'll kill your mom/dad/brother/sister/dog...
You'll ruin me if you tell.
I'll kill myself if you tell.
No one will understand our "special relationship."
I'll tell your friends you're queer.
You wanted it.
You enjoyed it.
You made me do it.

. . . and some, we told ourselves:

No one else ever did this stuff.
They'll think I'm queer.
No one can understand what I'm feeling.
They'll think I wanted it.
Asked for it.
Enjoyed it.

WHO you tell is pretty important.
I've told the wrong people.

Like, when I was fifteen, I told a school friend who saw it as an opportunity to "use" me, and told someone else who also "used" me.

Like when I was eighteen and I told a thirty-year-old father figure who offered to "help" me and trapped me and molested me too.

Like when I trusted someone with my writings, and they read them and read things into them and used them against me.

But I've also told the right people. Women friends who showed me a much needed gentle, caring side of women than I'd experienced. My business partner whose family has "adopted" me and one hundred percent trusts me with their children.

I remember telling my secret other times too, times that turned out very different from each other.

Rob lived in my apartment complex, and we developed a casual friendship. He was twenty and I was thirty-two. There was an unspoken sense of connection, as there always is among victims. Rob was fragile; he drank a lot. One night before I left on a business trip, he completely broke down. For him, the sense of finding a "big brother" who was safe also brought up feelings of danger and abandonment because I was leaving.

In the next few months, I felt the need to tell him where I'd been, though I wasn't sure he could handle it. He in turn shared his secret: repeat molestation. Memory blocks. Being molested by a fifty-year-old at an adult bookstore when he was eleven.

I continued to heal; Rob continued to run. He finally (and abruptly) severed any contact with me, which was very painful for me, as I felt (my victim blame thinking) it was my fault. (I knew I shouldn't have told!) Later I found he'd done it because he was becoming dependent and it terrified him. I understood.

Four years later, I ran into him, and we had a long late night talk. He wasn't doing well, was still drinking heavy and had attempted suicide. The reason he'd tried hurt to hear: he'd had sex on his twelve-year-old nephew. "I just did unto others what was done unto me," he said glibly. "Turn about's fair play." So the prey had become the predator. Known for my pit bull attitude toward molesters, I now could only cry. Yeah, I was angry. But he'd been my friend. I believe it's rare for a victim to become a Wolf, but it does happen. And I saw why. He never got help. He never stopped running. And now, he was passing on the nightmare. I can only pray he gets help before he kills himself or before victimizing becomes a way of life for him.

The next time I told was not individual. I'm a youth pastor with at risk teens, and I knew there was a good chance a lot of the kids I worked with had been molested. I remember when I was in a youth group as a kid, I was dying to find someone to trust and talk to about this, but there was no one to tell. So I decided to be up front with them after a few months and tell them I was a molestation survivor. My healing was strong enough that I could talk about it without shame or fear. I wanted to make it easy for them to talk, if they needed.

Two girls did and no boys. For several years. Then, one by one, some did. It took that many years to build enough trust for it. It wasn't me they didn't trust. It was their own hearts. They were ashamed. Weren't we all, at first? One only told me after consuming enough booze to nearly kill him, and he said, "I'll tell you once, and never again." And he hasn't. Another, fragile and wary, turned to drugs and sex to kill the pain, and it hurt to watch. I knew if he'd only talk, we could begin to mend his life. He told me a little and never again. Until he does start talking and facing what's there, he'll keep going until he self-destructs.

That's one of the best kept secrets of victims. We usually don't grow up and molest. We grow up and self-destruct. Talk-show mentality says to rapists, "So were you molested as a child?" Of course, a convicted molester will say that. Because it's part of the rationale. And yeah, sometimes they were. But just because some molesters were molested, doesn't mean the molested grow up to molest. We just fall apart, drug, and booze out, and disintegrate.

Unless we tell someone. Some time ago, I had breakfast with a friend who is like a blood brother to me. He'd told a little of his secret after we first met, but kept the rest inside. Then he got married and had kids, and now he confessed that he couldn't let go of it. He couldn't tell his wife. And it was complex, because he'd fondled someone a few years younger than himself when he was just barely into his teens, and he felt condemned, and evil, because he didn't understand that an eleven-year-old who fondles a nine-year-old is just repeating an action. He wasn't a "perpetrator."

The minute I started opening my heart and experience to him, his eyes clouded and tears began to fall. It really didn't matter WHAT I said, because he was responding deeply just because he had permission to talk about it without fear . . . or shame. Do you relate?

Like so many of us, the relief of his telling the secret was followed by a feeling of "I'm O.K. now that I talked, so it's over." So I told my friend to talk, and keep talking, talk to ME, I understand, and talk anytime you need to for as long as it takes. Don't bury it. You just scratched the surface. Open the wound, and let it begin to heal.

You'll feel scared and embarrassed and angry and unsure when you first tell the secret to someone. But do it anyway. Those who've walked in your shoes understand the need to keep talking and that there's no shame for things you were too young or too scared or too vulnerable to understand, or to stop.

Telling the secret is the only way to break the shame that binds your heart.

What Being Molested Cost Me

THE cost to a kid who gets molested is higher than most people know. It's too easy to minimize the damage by saying, "It's just one of those things," or "Get over it." Sexual violation is a violent thing even when it's not violent. It takes so much inside. After many years, I've taken notice of the losses (much of which has been healed and restored), and I want to tell you about it so you'll know.

It cost me my childhood. Repeated molestation blocked my memories, and what I did remember was covered with a haze of physical illness, stalking fear, repeat nightmares, and deep loneliness.

It cost me my ability to trust. I resented authority and feared adults so much I wouldn't go anyplace like a public rest room or swimming pool locker room because I'd get sick from the fear of what might happen.

It cost me my ability to be spontaneous. I kept such rigid control over my emotions, my body and my mind, that I couldn't laugh, I couldn't play, and being around kids who could made me feel sullen, angry, depressed, alone, left out.

It cost me my sanity. Shortly after the initial abuses, I was in a complete emotional dead zone; and one night, as I sat alone in a chair, my mind filled with filth and blasphemy, and tears streamed down my face, because I loved God and I couldn't stop this mental rape, and I just snapped after several days of this, and I started cursing, and smoking, and drinking, and I told God to give up on me because I was evil.

I was eleven.

It cost me my education potential. I was a brilliant child. Being molested cost me my ability to think without confusion, trance outs, and frustration. I couldn't concentrate. I could have been a straight A Valedictorian. Instead, by the time I finished High School, I was taking four basic classes and barely passed.

It cost me my identity. Being molested created such sexual and emotional confusion that I was an old man before I was fifteen and still a boy at thirty. I felt numb and removed, like I was not there, just a piece of property for others to use and discard.

It cost me my adolescence. Being molested made me afraid of adults, men, women, crowds, public places, challenges, fights and almost everything else including being scared to death I was gay and scared of all my emotions including anger and joy. I couldn't date, I didn't go to the prom, and alcohol was my only "friend." Being a kid is screwed up and scary enough, but I carried enough guilt and fear to take down ten normal adults.

It cost me time. Being molested started me running, and I ran and kept going until I crashed in my late twenties, and then it cost me time in recovering, facing hard truth, and healing.

It cost me family. Being molested crippled my heart enough to destroy any potential marriage or children.

God has restored most of what was taken, and more. But you need to know being molested is not a "get over it" thing. It's an evil robber whose damage goes deep and keeps taking until we can face it and start to heal.

Why We Don't Talk

I'M speaking on behalf of the many boys and men who have been molested. The "One In Six." We sit in your classrooms, worship in your churches, socialize at your parties, work at your businesses, and sleep in your beds.

We are a mystery to you. You probably sense something is "not quite right." We're distant and yet long for closeness, so we pull you in and then push you away. We drink too much and laugh too loud, and then suddenly retreat, fearing we'll call attention to ourselves—and then you'll know or at least start asking questions. And we never, EVER cry in front of you. It's too scary. We're too fragile. We're afraid if we get started, we'll never stop.

The littlest among us don't talk because we're scared. We know what they did to us is wrong, but they're big enough to hurt us or kill us if we tell. It may be our dad, and then if we tell they'll come and take him away, and it's our fault, and then our family will be gone, and who's gonna take care of us then? Besides, he said he's sorry and he loves me. That's why he said he did it, 'cause I'm special, and if I tell and he leaves, I won't be special anymore.

If he's an uncle or cousin or brother or Grampa, no one will believe me; and they'll say it wasn't what I thought it was and he didn't mean it that way and it's probably my imagination. Plus he gave me stuff and paid attention to me; so I have to do stuff with him.

If he's a teacher, I won't tell because you're supposed to respect and obey teachers; plus he says my school friends will find out if I tell and hate me.

If he's a priest or a minister, I won't tell because he's God's authority and I'm supposed to trust him and he said it's O.K. with God what we're doing and it would be wrong not to trust God's man.

Adolescent boys. We don't talk because it's too complicated. Sex is new, and it feels good. This older man says he's my friend. He says all boys do it, so it's O.K., right? Even though it doesn't feel right. He spends a lot of time and money on me, and I trust him. He's older, he knows better, right? He says Greek and Roman teachers did this stuff with their boy

students to teach them how to be a man. He makes me feel like an adult because he lets me smoke and drink and smoke pot and look at his pornography and sex videos and stuff. He says it's normal to get turned on by it and that he knows how to take care of it for me. He says we're not gay or anything, and he told me about some other guys I know who he says do it too, so maybe its all right because I know they've got girlfriends and everything, so they're not gay. But I don't tell because he says people will think I am, and if my parents found out they'd be mad as hell. He tells me it's normal because guys just can't get enough sex, and it's unhealthy not to; and he says he knows I enjoy him doing sex on me because I can't help responding.

I don't tell because he took pictures of me and says if they "get out" everyone will know I'm a pervert (even though he says he knows I'm not). He even had me do a video with some other kids and even paid us, so I can't tell now, 'cause they'll put me in jail for it. At least that's what he says.

I don't tell because I'm confused and hurting. If it's normal, how come I feel so dirty? How come it feels good sometimes, but how come I hate myself afterward? He tells me it's not "queer"; so how come I feel like it is? Why don't I just tell him to stop? Why am I so afraid of him? Because if he gets mad, he says I'll be the one who's sorry. What does he mean by that? I hate him, but if he starts coming on to another kid I feel scared and mad and rejected and abandoned. No one understands the power he's got over me to confuse me, make me feel good, scare me, make me feel important, power to trap me. I won't tell because there's no way in hell anyone would believe I didn't want this to happen somehow, or understand me, or love me. I'm just a piece of property, and everyone will think I asked for it or if I was a real man I would've been able to stop him. They don't understand. I don't tell because I'm ashamed. And I'm afraid. And no matter how bad all this is, it's better than you knowing what I did.

Men don't talk for a lot of reasons. We don't talk because

people don't believe boys and teens can be raped. We don't tell because you'll laugh and joke about us behind our backs. You'll think we're less than men. We don't tell because we've still got a little boy and a terrified adolescent inside us that have sworn to keep our mouths shut no matter how much it hurts us.

We don't talk because we can't stand another "get over it" lecture. We don't talk because our fears, no matter how unreasonable, tell us we'll lose our jobs, our wives, our kids if we do. We're scared if we talk that you'll treat us like we're different than everyone else, and scared you'll treat us like we're the same, and we're not! We don't talk because men should handle things alone and boys don't do stuff like that—and we know you can't handle the thought that they really do and is he gonna molest my kids???

We don't talk because we don't trust; and believe me, that trust has to be earned. We were betrayed before. You have to prove you won't do it again.

Predator Radar—Then & Now

UNFORTUNATELY, being molested for me was a repeated experience and went on into late adolescence. I was a gaping wound; predators know that kind of thing. Like a wolf that's had a taste of blood, they can sniff out a wounded kid. They're "easy."

Now if you haven't been molested, you won't understand how a boy or teen kid who was molested can "let it happen" more than once. Well, it's like you're paralyzed. When you're little, and a stronger, older teen or adult molests you, you're in panic fear and go into total shock and paralysis. You can't move. Your mind is saying, "They can't be doing this to me," your body is responding to the sexual stimulation, but your heart and body are frozen and unable to stop them.

Unhealed, the next predator finds you easily, and makes you relive the nightmare. If you're not willing to accept the reality of repeat molestation, don't try to help a victim of it. They'll know in a second if you're thinking, "He could have just said no or kicked them or something."

Besides the satanic abuse and child pornography I was forced into as a child, I was later initiated by an older boy when I was about nine, and it continued until I was fourteen, which is also the year I was raped by someone who picked me up hitch-hiking. At sixteen, it happened again at work, and at eighteen an older man "took me under his wing," played father figure to me, let me move in with him to help me through school, and molested me for three months.

I suffered horribly with guilt and confusion for years. If you haven't been molested and you're struggling to accept someone who has been molested more than once, you have no idea what it's like to hate yourself so much for "letting it happen" again. Only in the last ten years could I accept that I was just responding to the poison of predator seduction and paralyzation and conditioning. Now I know. Now I can smell a predator a mile away, no matter how slick they are. I can feel him sniffing for fresh blood.

Several predators were experts at emotional manipulation and guilt. "If you tell, I'll kill myself!" (Yeah? Go for it.) I fell for this one: "It's something all kids do." (No it ain't. Not with adults. Not with people like you).

Breaking the sexual entrapment was hard. But I didn't realize I tended to attract ALL power grabbers looking for someone to control. Most of my relationships were people who were drawn to my "hurt puppy" look, and developed a friendship where they had total control and emotional power. I did what THEY wanted, I went where THEY wanted to go; and if I got angry at not being considered, they got upset, and said I was ungrateful for all they did for me!

I even got trapped by a counselor that showered me with "love" and gifts and money. He said I never let him love me. Maybe I didn't. It was at a time when my new "radar" was being installed, and maybe I could sense there was going to be a big price tag to this relationship if I let him get too close to me. I knew there was going to be a catch. He wanted to "love" me, "counsel" me, "take care" of me—translation: "Control" me. (Note: Not everyone who wants to do these things for us has power motives; that's why having sharp radar is important.)

When I finally confronted him, he went NUTS. Cried. Cajoled. Left. He followed up with a letter which tore me to shreds.

I returned everything. And I forgave him, and ended the relationship, and vowed that this would be the last time I'd ever get trapped by anyone with a predator's scent, sexually or emotionally. And it was.

I LEARNED TO TAKE CARE OF MYSELF.

HAPPY IS THE MAN THAT FINDETH WISDOM, AND THE MAN THAT GETTETH UNDER-STANDING. PROVERBS 3:13

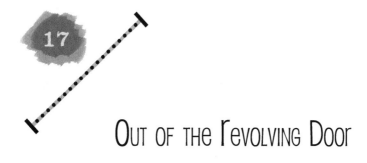

Out of the revolving Door

I had to break free.

I was "used." The ones who used me owned me. I had no choice, no rights, no control.

That's why, after the first one, it was so easy for the next one to use me, and the next one, and the next . . . They knew the walls were broken down. They knew I couldn't /wouldn't fight back. I didn't know how. I didn't think I could.

After years of going through the revolving door of predators, I stopped it. Now no one touched my body without my permission. No one used my body for their own sick needs.

But no one prepared me for non-sexual predators.

I didn't know then that sexual abuse of a child is just the extreme end of adults who were self-centered, power-addicted, and needed to control someone smaller, someone weaker and vulnerable to make them feel strong and good about themselves. In control.

I didn't know then that a relationship doesn't have to be sexually abusive to be destructive.

I didn't know that the most valuable walls were still broken down in me—the ones that draw boundaries, that say no, that require respect and sensitivity and consideration and shared giving.

One day I realized that most of my friendships were demeaning, demanding, one way, contingent on my performance, my compliance, my back seat position, my weakness, and my unimportance compared to the "important" needs of the other.

And I realized that every one of these friends were either predator in nature, vampiristic, or unhealed (and unwilling to heal) molestation victims themselves.

So I stopped dancing. And one by one, they whined, they attacked, and then they let go, as if I had never mattered to them at all. Because I didn't in their world, people only existed as stage props to make them look and feel good or to serve their own needs and pleasures. They got back into the revolving door, looking for a new prop in human form. Names optional; compliance and passivity a must.

And there they are still

Dancing mostly alone,

And I, out of the door, was embraced by those who never learned to dance.

CHARITY SUFFERETH LONG, AND IS KIND; CHARITY ENVIETH NOT; CHARITY VAUNTETH NOT ITSELF, IS NOT PUFFED UP, DOTH NOT BEHAVE ITSELF UNSEEMLY, SEEKETH NOT HER OWN, IS NOT EASILY PROVOKED, THINKETH NO EVIL. I CORINTHIANS 13:4-5

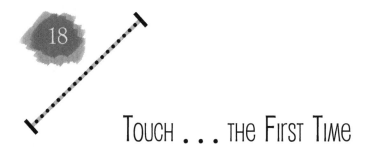

TOUCH ... THE FIRST TIME

THERE'S one issue I rarely hear talked about concerning male molestation survivors. It's probably too sensitive. It's about touch.

Now, everybody needs to be loved, and touched, and held. You die if you don't have that.

For male survivors, it's not that easy. Because who touches you, and for what reason, are always painful issues. For a lot of us, our first genuine touch and affection and attention was mixed with genital stimulation, sensual pleasure, and counterfeit "love."

For us who suffered repeated molestation, a pattern, a horrible trapdoor pattern emerged. We were conditioned. If we were touched by a molester, (1) We froze, (2) We felt powerless, (3) We felt wanted, desired, liked, (4) We got erections, (5) We were fondled and caressed, and (6) we were forced to perform sex on our molester. It can be ten times as complicated and confusing if this first molester forced us to experience our first orgasm. It's wrong . . . but I feel good feelings.. he's hurting me . . . but I trust him . . . but he's an adult, and I'm just a little kid . . . What a nightmare! We end up feeling like trash to be used and discarded. And the shame and fear is overwhelmed by fear of the molester's anger, or by the fear that he will not love us and reject and abandon us and we may lose the only person who's ever showed us any attention or "love."

If the molestation happened as a child (and was not violent), we tend to grow up to crave affection, approval and being liked. If it happened as an adolescent, we've got to deal with the confusion of having sexually new experiences exploited by an expert molester who knows how to bring intense and overwhelming and addictive pleasure out of a sexually awakened and naive young kid who knows no better and is unaware that this explosive experience will change him forever.

If it happened as a child and a teenager, it's living hell.

Do you know why many of us end up promiscuous with women? We've got to prove the experiences we can't talk about didn't make us "queer." Funny how we're always paying the price for someone else's crime. Some of us even end up promiscuous with men, or as street hustlers, not because we're gay, but because it's the only thing we knew. We were conditioned.

My molestations were by both men and women, some violent and some "affectionate" and seducing. So I ended up neither promiscuous nor aggressive—just flat paralyzed. Unable to touch. Unable to be touched, or to stop from being touched.

I was devoid of any touch that was real or healthy or nonsexual until I was fifteen. The walls of hate and fear kept everybody away by then.

I became a Christian that year, and my whole life changed. God became a safe place for me. People, well that was another matter! Despite my fears, a boy and girl my age befriended me, and slowly the walls crumbled.

It all came crashing down one day after church when we'd gone to one of their homes for lunch. They wanted to pray with me, and they believed in putting their arms around each others' shoulders when they did, and when they did this to me, I was suddenly hit by an overpowering sexual rush. I ran crying into the woods, feeling dirty and ashamed and evil. "Why, God?" I didn't expect an answer, but I got one: You're not dirty or evil. Sex is all you've known. You responded to touch with sexual feelings because you've never been touched without sex being part of it. You will heal. You will know that touch is good, and clean, and it doesn't mean sex is next." I did heal, and soon the ability to hug someone or be close physically without an erotic "Pavlovian" response was mine.

The fact that great healing can come through non-sexual affection from the same gender that abused us can't be understated. Finding that among recovering molestation survivors is a godsend. Not finding it leaves you untrusting, always on the attack, and always doubting your own needs, feelings, sexuality, selfhood.

For married men, it's pretty rough. Sex, as a friend told me, is a sacrifice. You end up always having to be in control, and if your wife is aggressive, you freeze if she desires sex, you read "demand" and think, "I'll just lay down, be a victim, and get it over with;" and you resent it, and she senses it, and she's hurt, and feels rejected, and resents it too. How do you explain that being desired for sex can make you feel dirty and powerless, controlled and FIVE-YEARS-OLD?

Learning touch as healthy, healing, and necessary takes time. But don't give up—God can heal even the deepest wounds and change touch from something sinister, painful, frightening, and awful into something warm, healing, holy, and good.

73

IT FELT GOOD . . . SORT OF

I would be lying to you, and you'd be lying to yourself, if we said all the molestation was physically painful. It wasn't. (Predators know that, and know how to use that against us, to condition us.)

This is the most painful for male survivors: To admit that some of it felt good. But until we do, we're not being real, and we're not going to heal. Because in admitting it felt good sometimes, you'll finally come to see how evil and wrong it was for the molester to take such a good, God given capacity for pleasure and ruin it for us because they wanted it for themselves.

What happens when you wash a little boy's penis? Regardless of age he gets an erection. Even babies. It's normal, and biological, and good. It's a first step in physical growth that will lead to growing up, and puberty, and sexual awakening, and perhaps marriage and children.

It's a precious gift.

A gift that was stolen from us.

A little boy should not know the sensation of an adult mouth on his penis. Because to the boy, it feels very good. It's a biological reaction. But we're not old enough to know that, or understand that this adult is hurting us deeply. We could not

NOT respond! But then, they knew that. And so we were split in two; we knew it was wrong, so why did it have to feel good? So we blame ourselves: Our bodies are to blame. It's our fault. We're sick. Evil. We wanted it. (That is also the favorite theory of organized predator groups pushing for legalized sex with any age.)

A child wants warm feelings and affection. We NEED it. So an adult gives us warm feelings, stroking our bodies while they provide warm body feelings, and they call it "loving" us. And we accept this love, because we trust them, and we grow dependent on them to give us these feelings, which we now can't separate from fondling and sex, because now in our minds it's the only way we can really know we are "loved."

It felt good. Sort of. Then why do we feel so empty, so lonely, so lost? Because we know in an instinctive, God given way that this is not love. This is rape. And it's left us confused, and longing for that "special touch" and attention to know that we're worth something, that we're special, and we're dependent on the person who is molesting us to tell us this is normal, that we're normal; and we're afraid we'll never be normal again, and we feel lost and abandoned when they go on and leave us behind to bleed in secret.

We are orphans in the storm. Please hold us and ask nothing in return.

Only then will we know we're safe.

> SUFFER THE LITTLE CHILDREN TO COME UNTO ME, AND FORBID THEM NOT: FOR OF SUCH IS THE KINGDOM OF GOD. VERILY I SAY UNTO YOU, WHOSOEVER SHALL NOT RECEIVE THE KINGDOM OF GOD AS A LITTLE CHILD, HE SHALL NOT ENTER THEREIN. AND HE TOOK THEM UP IN HIS ARMS, PUT HIS HANDS UPON THEM, AND BLESSED THEM. MARK 10: 13-16

aUTHORITY

MALE survivors sometimes become pushovers, compliant men who will do anything to please those in authority. It probably comes from fear and longing for approval, which probably stems from the enormous power those who molested us had over us as children. We were property. We did what we were told, without question. If we let them use us, they seemed to "love" us more and pay more attention to us; so when we got older, it became a way of life: Compliance means love, acceptance, maybe gifts, and it means we won't get hurt physically by saying no.

A friend was a little shocked when I told him how, when I was picked up hitchhiking at fourteen, driven to a remote place, and cornered into sex by a man twice my age, I actually removed my own clothes so he could rape me. Why? Because I knew he was going to do it anyway, so I did it because (1) If I didn't, he might kill me, and (2) I wanted to have some control over this nightmare he was inflicting on me. In his mind, I'm sure, I was a "willing, consensual boy," but truth was, I was saving my life and preserving what little sense of control and dignity I had left in such a twisted situation.

So compliance rarely means for us that we're just nice guys. It means we're afraid, and if we just do whatever you ask, maybe you'll back off, leave us alone, not hurt us.

But it backfires for a lot of us, and the rage over being used becomes big time rebellion against all authority. So a lot of us push the envelope of danger, run through jobs like sox, and get angry when anyone tells us what to do.

In my own life, I could see it in the way I changed as a child. I was obedient, polite, and my room was always neat and orderly. (None of that is bad!) Then, coinciding with being abused, I started smoking, drinking, smarting off to teachers, vandalizing, and my neat orderly room became a total wreck.

I collapsed inside, because the safe world where you obey adults and trust your neighbors and you'll be loved and rewarded ended up in sodomy and pornographic abuse and the death of believing in adults as safe and caring and kind.

At eleven, I told my scoutmaster to take my uniform and shove it you know where after he demanded I change into it for the trip home from a campout. He thought I was just a rebel. He didn't know how degrading being told to take off my clothes by anyone was for me.

I don't advocate rebellion, unless it's against abuse, or manipulation, or injustice done to innocent kids. But those of us who survived molestation need to see that behind the rebellion is often a rage because we lost control of our body to a molester, and that rage and rebellion is a way of warding off danger and intrusion. It's a cover for the devastating loss of faith in authority figures. We need to begin to peel back the onion and get to the core hurt and betrayal, get the rage out safely, cry out the betrayal, and learn new ways of recognizing misplaced anger and begin building a safe world where you can learn to trust authority again.

There are a lot of pastors and church leaders out there that need to hear this. Responding well to spiritual authority may be the hardest of all for us, because we may be mad at God for what happened to us. Please don't glibly write off kids who are "in rebellion." Yeah, some rebel because they're just selfish and out of relationship with God. But a lot of us are just scared. Why should we trust your authority? Didn't we once trust, and weren't we shattered by the ones claiming they were the authority, the adult, so we just needed to obey their wishes to rape us?

If you want us to respond to true authority, we must first respond to your love, your patient kindness, your desire to know us and see beyond the anger into the hurt and let us know we can trust you. Then maybe we can let go of the rebellion and learn to know the love of a God who knows our hurt and whose Son suffered it all. Be our window, not our judge.

Feeling My Skin

BEING raped and molested was so fragmenting that I seemed to walk out of my body, and I've never quite returned. Children should not experience forced sexual feelings. They should have their own bodies to themselves, to be able to experience good touch, and tickling, and warm love. They took that away. Being raped made normal body functions a nightmare of humiliation, so much so that having to use the rest-room is a shameful act, never done with anyone around. Oral sex disconnected me from that part of me God designed for pleasure and procreation. Oral rape said, "This is not mine. It's theirs." Every embrace became a threat, every caress a violation. It said, "Only I can make you feel." The hated touch created an empty shell of a body that could not respond to even my own touch.

I want to feel my skin. It's got nothing to do with sex. I want to be able to touch my face, and know we are connected. But I only feel an alien sensation of deadness.

Damn those! Who made me dependent on their abusive hands to feel anything at all.

I cannot feel the moment. I am running inside, like I did then. So now, if I am hurt, I go numb, and only awaken to the pain months later. People think I'm strong when I pass through a death, or rejection, or a loss so stoically. They don't see me months later when I without cause break apart alone, crying in fits of hurt and rage over long past pain or bereavement. This is what they did; they made me run, and go numb, because you can't cry when they're raping you and for God's sake, don't FEEL. If you respond to pleasure, that will only encourage them to go on.

So I can't feel a warm breeze, or warm shower water on a cold winter morning, or smell soft scents, because it's too dangerous. They might come back and see that I'm alive and enjoying the pleasure of sense, and take it for themselves.

Just play dead.

Then they'll go away.

> MY HEART IS SORE PAINED WITHIN ME: AND THE TERRORS OF DEATH ARE FALLEN UPON ME. FEARFULNESS AND TREMBLING ARE COME UPON ME, AND HORROR HATH OVERWHELMED ME. AND I SAID, OH THAT I HAD WINGS LIKE A DOVE! FOR THEN WOULD I FLY AWAY, AND BE AT REST.
> PSALM 55: 4-6

Teddy Bear or Tiger?

WE survivors usually go one of two ways. We either become aggressive and act out on others, or we are passive and become doormats.

As a former Doormat, I'd like to tell you how I got off the floor. It wasn't easy. Like a lot of boys, I was shy and good natured, easy to please and very gentle. The abuse turned that set of good qualities into passivity and self-destruction.

I was taught never to get mad. But anger is part of us. You can't remove it. You can only direct it. So instead of being mad at being abused, mad at the abusers, I turned it inside and got mad at myself. Hated myself. Hated the little boy who "let it happen," so I hated my gentle side. But I couldn't hide it.

That's what attracted predators to me. They knew I was too "nice" to say no. (Some even molested me saying they were helping me not to hate myself.)

So the duality was killing me. There was the "teddy bear" exterior (most of it real, some just a "maybe they won't see me" defense), but there was a rage inside. I denied I was angry. To this day, when someone says, "Are you angry with me?," I fight not to lie. Because "it's wrong to get mad." And, I was afraid—

afraid that if I ever tapped into the well of rage, I'd lose control, I'd destroy things, I'd kill someone.

I didn't know it was normal to be angry—that it was necessary to healing to be angry about being used for someone else's sexual gratification and power pleasure. As a Christian, it was a great relief to realize (1) Jesus got angry, (2) God gets angry, and if we're made in His image and likeness, anger is a part of us He made, and (3) the Bible says to "Be ye angry, and sin not: let not the sun go down upon your wrath" (Ephesians 4:26). The way I read it, it's saying, don't stuff it or deny it, deal with it! Resolve it! Anger turned inward can't be God's will because it leads to promiscuity, substance abuse, and self-hate; for the believing heart who has Christ dwelling inside, Scripture tell us that we are the temple of God—we should cherish and nurture the temple God gave us to live in (I Corinthians 3:16).

First, I dealt with the anger in a private way. It started out by a therapy session in which I was encouraged to beat the heck out of a pillow named after the current person I was mad at, until feathers flew. Exhausting, but not very helpful. It didn't really lessen my anger. And it's not as easy for some of us, like "I hate the person who molested me." Because sometimes for us, it's "I hate them, I love them, I need them, I'm afraid of them." So I stopped naming my inanimate pillows, and switched to cheap glassware thrown at my backyard wall instead.

Finally, I settled on my journal. A lot of times, I didn't even know why I was angry, or what set it off. So I just wrote. Anything. I was so out of touch with my feelings, it was all "I think, I saw, I did, I realized." It took a long time to get to "I'm feeling," and be able to let the emotions pour out. When they did, it was Katy Bar The Door. My language was graphic and bitter, hateful and enraged. I feared the expression of it because I didn't want to face it. "It's wrong to hate." Well, it had to be there in me anyway, or it wouldn't have come out on paper at all! The point isn't whether it's wrong or not. The point is: IS

IT IN MY HEART? To deny its presence is to let it remain a hidden cancer. Yes, there are ungodly feelings and hate in there. But there's also some justified anger and hurt. You'll never know the difference between them until you get all the cards on the table, all the feelings in front of you in writing. Only then can you let go and be cleansed of destructive emotions and learn to use and cherish the healthy ones. See?

As I wrote, I discovered a great truth: Behind the hate was a world of hurt. Behind the anger was a lot of fear. Hate defended me from more hurt and from facing my hurt.

Some of the anger was a way of keeping people away (so I wouldn't get molested anymore), and it kept me from facing the vulnerable, gentle side of me.

The more I wrote, the more clearly I saw things. I could see myself—the "public" self, the "private" self. The private one was enraged and confused. The public one danced to any tune just to be liked; the private one was furious because he didn't want to dance and hated the hypocrisy. The public one joked, was cynical, never said no to any demand or expectation; the private one cried, longed to be real and communicate honestly and was tired of being everyone's doormat.

Finally, the inside guy won. I think it started when a friend observed the backflips I did to please people and said, "Why don't you get off the dance floor and go home?" Yeah, but HOW?

Well, first I had to accept that dancing takes two, and the people I felt most obligated to please were either manipulative and slightly predator in nature, or reminded me of someone who molested me. (I was afraid not to do what they said. We know what happened when we tried to say no as boys.)

So I just stopped dancing. I cut off people who just used me and self-centered *friends* who weren't capable of having a two-way relationship. I stopped doing things for people just because I'd feel guilty if I didn't. (I had so many commitments going before this that I had to set up an appointment just to see myself!) I took note of the people who put guilt on me, whined or got angry if I didn't respond or do what they wanted, and eased myself out of their lives.

Being a public person, I learned another gem: Beware of those who praise you too much, because they've got a sharp knife waiting when you turn your back and say, "Sorry, I can't."

So I ended up with more time and started to really enjoy it when I did help people out. And, my real friends understood when I said "no." And, I don't miss the others that much.

By letting the Tiger out some, the Teddy Bear in me felt safer and more protected. They need each other. Too much Tiger is dangerous and hurtful. Too much Teddy Bear is unsafe and unrealistic. Together, they're the real me. I do get angry. But I also cry. I can say no, but I also give my whole heart when I help others.

Before, the Tiger tore me up, and the Teddy Bear had tire marks on his face. (It reminds me of the ultimate illustrated sermon: A friend saw a Ziggy "Please Love Me" doll with his arms outstretched, flatter than a pancake on the open road.)

Now, they walk together with dignity, love, and strength. To my friends, I can be the warmest hug and a sheltering tree.

But manipulators, predators, and perpetrators beware this Teddy Bear has CLAWS!

Letting Go

NONE of us want to be professional victims. When we first begin recovering, it's so incredible to tell our story among those who have been there, who understand. It's safe for the first time, and so the long road to healing begins.

But none of us want to stay there, to let our abuse become our identity. Yes, it will always be part of us, and that's good, because others need to hear our story. But to cling to that identity is to eventually die inside, because our recovery and disclosure is like good medicine that's used to help us get through pain after surgery. Eventually we have to lay it down because otherwise we will become addicted to the very thing that helped us get better.

I think we may always need to talk, to find shelter. But true healing means we eventually take on life, and integrate with the normal of life, and no longer are trapped by what happened. Our abuse becomes another facet of our lives.

No one can tell you when that letting go begins, but it is gradual, and soon you'll feel the discomfort of that old identity as an every-day workshirt and decide to put it on hangers and just put it on when you need it. When it feels comfortable to do it.

If you're like me, you're sick of the "victim bandwagon" that has become our culture, where everything from a simple spanking to being asked for a date is called abuse. It's insulting to us who have suffered real abuse, and to those real victims of sexual abuse and damage, especially the little ones. The more I saw this, the more I longed to just be known for who I am, not for what I endured.

Part of the letting go for me was taking responsibility for my life and actions. Yes, there was a time I could clearly see that "I did that because I was molested." But it became an excuse after a while. Then a little voice in my head said, "Yeah, but now you know better. So admit you blew it. You're an adult now. You know the game, you can avoid the traps. You don't have to respond as a victim anymore. Respond as a victor."

It was a tough transition from blaming my abuse to accepting my responsibility. I had to let it go. I had to accept blame for my failures and bad reactions without reaching back and saying, "I did it because . . ." Because that was then and this is now. In accepting that responsibility, it became easier to recognize my potential response to a triggering situation based on the past and say, "Change course. Steer clear. You can do it differently now."

Because the only way to regain our dignity is to say, "I'm not a victim now. I'm in charge." Because the ultimate victory of our molesters would be if we don't break the pattern of helplessness and defeat and self-medication and self-destruction.

You can destroy their power by saying, "No more. I don't have to live as a victim anymore."

Letting go, it's something you learn through brave effort and honesty and the courage to find a new identity away from the abuse. Be patient. It takes time. But let it go.

Living well, as they say, is the ultimate payback for those who took our childhood away.

Letter to a Molester

To Whoever You Are:

Your name doesn't matter, for to me, you were just a stranger in a Volkswagen who gave me a ride. And to you, I was just a number, a cute fourteen-year-old anonymous kid, one of God knows how many.

I think about it a lot. Even though you weren't the first to molest me, you probably did more damage than most. At fourteen, I was just beginning to explore my sexuality, and I was vulnerable. All my sexual antennas were active, but then you knew that, didn't you? That's why you picked kids like me. We were easy prey; we were little enough to feel scared and overpowered by you, old enough to sexually respond to what you did.

I hated you, and I have forgiven you. Because to not forgive you meant I always lived for you, thought about you, lived in the darkness of what you did and longed for vengeance. Five years after you raped me, I saw you while I was driving, and pressed the accelerator to the floor to kill you. You were still driving the same Volkswagen. Only God's grace pulled back my foot and let you live. And then I knew that you bound me still. And so I forgave not because it was rational but because it was killing me, not because you deserve it but because I needed to let it go. Forgive means "give forth" and so I gave back the chains you put me in. I don't hate you anymore. I feel nothing at all, but sadness, for what you took from me—that I can never reclaim my adolescence.

I do pray for you for repentance, if possible. And if not, for imprisonment, not to punish you (for you must loath your every breath) but to stop you. Because if you raped me, I wasn't the first, and certainly not the last.

I pray for all the kids you raped like me. You cannot know what you took, what you destroyed. The walking wounded see your face, feel your evil touch, and blame themselves.

I wish I could tell them it wasn't them. You knew exactly how it's done. They were powerless, and paralyzed, and afraid.

They probably still are.

Letter to Joel

DEAR Joel:
You were just ten when I met you. You'd been molested.
You were old. You were aware. You knew too much. But you
wouldn't talk about it. I understand; I was an adult. A man
and men molested you. Why should you trust me?

But you did trust me, a little. Because the last time I saw
you, you came bounding up to me and hugged me and let me
hold you, and you were not afraid. It's a gift I'll treasure forever,
because I know how hard it is to trust anyone again.

We are the same, you and me. Only age separates us. You
are an old man inside, seeing more than a little boy should
ever see. And I am a little boy, still believing in rainbows and
cotton candy and warm hugs. It is he that reaches out to you.

If I could, I'd go back and stop what was done to you. I'd
fight them, do anything I had to—just so you knew you weren't
alone. Someone cares that you hurt.

But I can't, so I can only love you from a distance, and
not pry into that painful place so scary, so degrading, so dark.
I don't expect your trust. I know I have to earn it. So every
time I see you, everything I do will say, "You're safe, it's O.K.,"

and we'll play nerf football and fly kites like before, and I'll try to show you a man who's survived the same wounds as you, who is gentle, and strong, and real. That's all I can do, until you know I really can be trusted with your most awful secrets. I promise you, I'll never hurt you. I'll never make fun of you. I'll get to you wherever you are if you need me. Because I need you, Joel, to tell me there's hope for tomorrow in your eyes, and I'll know my pain was not for nothing, that I can give you shelter and hope in your violent storm.

Your friend always,
Greg

GREATER LOVE HATH NO MAN THAN THIS, THAT A MAN LAY DOWN HIS LIFE FOR HIS FRIENDS. JOHN 15:13

I've Got Nothing to Prove

I feel good in my skin now. I own my body, and my heart. I no longer fear predators, sexual or emotional, because no one gets past this gate without express permission and suitable credentials. It is they who now steer clear of me. That is as it should be; for I have taken back my worth, and I am not afraid to confront the manipulators and expose the predators. Their time is over. Mine has begun.

I've reclaimed my anger and made it constructive. I've regained my innocence and no longer fear my needs, or my heart.

I no longer have to justify my existence, or seek to disappear in a corner to make room for more worthy people, or defend myself from ghosts and shadows. I am free.

I can speak freely of my past without caring what others think, knowing it is only humane and decent for others to accept my experience, and not doing so is a reflection on their fears and inadequacy of love, not on me.

I alone felt this pain. I alone. I was there. I survived against all odds. I'm proud to have made it. I'm humbled because only

God could have made me well and whole again. I am real, and kind, and loving, and intact.

I've got nothing left to prove.

The LORD is my shepherd; I shall not want. He maketh me to lie down in green pastures: he leadeth me beside the still waters. He restoreth my soul: he leadeth me in the paths of righteousness for his name's sake. Psalm 23:1-3

I've Got to Do Something

WHY did I survive? Why am I alive? For so long, I struggled to go on amidst the pain and the abandonment and the fear. But I made it. Why? I'm glad I did, but what good was all the pain if all I did was survive? I want to do more than survive. There has to be more.

Maybe I started to know at seventeen when I met Johnny, who was thirteen. Trust came slowly, and so did the story about his Boy Scout leader molesting him. I've never forgotten that shy, fragile hurting boy. I never will.

Only in the last decade did I understand. I've walked through crowds and gatherings and youth groups and congregations for years, and I sensed them there, the one in six; I saw flashes of pain-filled eyes, longing to reach another but bound by crippling fear.

Then came the children, injured children with no visible scars but a hollow echo of a child's laughter like a ghost in their hearts followed by a scream of desperation no one could hear.

Then I knew, I had to do something. No matter what the cost. No matter what people thought.

I longed for years for a voice of my own kind to speak, to

say, "You're not alone, I've been there too," but no one came, so I knew I'd have to be a voice for others. I saw myself in each one, felt their sorrow, and held their trust as sacred. I always will. They are the bravest company I know.

So I'll keep speaking because there are more. I had to do something. Because God wastes nothing, not even our loneliest sorrows and worst devastations.

Wouldn't you have to do something, too?

> BLESSED BE GOD, EVEN THE FATHER OF OUR LORD JESUS CHRIST, THE FATHER OF MERCIES, AND THE GOD OF ALL COMFORT: WHO COMFORTETH US IN ALL OUR TRIBULATION, THAT WE MAY BE ABLE TO COMFORT THEM WHICH ARE IN ANY TROUBLE, BY THE COMFORT WHEREWITH WE OURSELVES ARE COMFORTED OF GOD. II CORINTHIANS 1:3-4

EPILOGUE

DEAR Mark:

It's midnight, and I just finished this book on sexual abuse. I think you would have liked it. I kind of wrote it for you, because you never grew up to help me with it. I know you would have. Wouldn't that have been something, for us to have both survived, and grown up together, and been a team? We could have helped the others together. I'm crying, because you're still so much a part of me, and how I miss you. So I'm writing this for both of us.

I hope you know I haven't forgotten you. I see you so clear, your blond hair and deep blue eyes, and the cocky, mischievous smile that made the light dance in your eyes. You were my hero, you know? My big brother, my bes' buddy, my defender. I wanted to be like you. I guess you were too good for this stinking evil world anyway. Who knows? Maybe if you'd lived, they'd have ruined you, too. I'm glad they couldn't make me forget your face. I never want to forget you. I had to for awhile, I know you understand. I just wasn't strong enough to keep remembering you died. I was so lost, Mark, I needed you with me so bad; they just killed you, and I had this big gaping hole in my heart, and I just couldn't handle it until a few years ago, because when they killed you, they took away the one safe place I ever had, the one person I knew really loved me. Now I'll never forget you, I promise.

What with the drugs and all, I almost couldn't remember,

but I broke through. But even when I was too screwed up and shattered to remember everything, I still dreamed about you and wondered why you were gone, why you left me. I never really forgot.

Listen, about the sex stuff and the pictures. It wasn't your fault, mine neither. They made us. And you never, ever hurt me; I saw you cry, I know. Even when we had to do the stuff they told us to, I knew you were trying to protect me. I never blamed you. And it was like even in the end, you saved me, because you died, not me. That's why I promise I'll always remember you. "One brother in exchange for another." Man, I wish you'd lived, not me, but maybe God knew I'd be stronger and tell them about it, about you.

They're dead now, Mark. They can't hurt you and me anymore—or kids like us.

But there's others, so I'm going to keep fighting them for both of us. I know you'd want me to. I won't let your sacrifice be for nothing. And everywhere I go, I'll tell them about you, about us, because I want people to know you were here, that your life meant something.

So I'm ending this book with a note from me to you, because you're part of everything I do. Sometimes I hurt, and if I just can remember your smile and laugh (remember how it could make me laugh no matter how bad I felt?), then I'll be O.K. I miss you Mark, and I love you, and one day I'll walk out of here and be Home, and if I see you standing there, I'll come running; you know I will, because that's how much you mean to me.

Until then, Mark, I hold you in my heart,
Blood Brothers Forever,
WolfBoy.

Hope

Let not your heart be troubled: ye believe in God, believe also in me. In my Father's house are many mansions: if it were not so, I would have told you. I go to prepare a place for you. And if I go and prepare a place for you, I will come again, and receive you unto myself; that where I am, there ye may be also. And whither I go ye know, and the way ye know. Thomas saith unto him, Lord, we know not whither thou goest; and how can we know the way? Jesus saith unto him, I am the way, the truth, and the life: no man cometh unto the Father, but by me. John 14: 1-6

Appendix #1
Child Sexual Abuse—Disclosures

Among victims of sexual abuse, the inability to trust is pronounced, which also contributes to secrecy and non-disclosure. **Source: Courtois & Watts, 1982.**

Children often fail to report because of the fear that disclosure will bring consequences even worse than being victimized again. The victim may fear consequences from the family, feel guilty for consequences to the perpetrator, and may fear subsequent retaliatory actions from the perpetrator. **Sources: Berlinger & Barbieri, 1984; Groth, 1979; Swanson & Biaggio, 1985.**

Victims may be embarrassed or reluctant to answer questions about the sexual activity. **Source: Berlinger & Barbieri, 1984.**

Victims may also have a feeling that "something is wrong with me," and that the abuse is their fault. **Sources: Johnson, 1987; Tsai & Wagner, 1978.**

In addition to "sexual guilt," there are several other types of guilt associated with the abuse, which include feeling different from peers, harboring vengeful and angry feelings toward both parents, feeling responsible for the abuse, feeling guilty about reporting the abuse, and bringing disloyalty and disruption to the family. Any of these feelings of guilt could outweigh the decision of the victim to report, the result of which is the secret may remain intact and undisclosed. **Source: Courtois & Watts, 1982; Tsai & Wagner, 1978.**

A child's initial denial of sexual abuse should not be the sole basis of reassurance that abuse did not occur. Virtually all investigative protocols are designed to respond to only those children who have disclosed. Policies and procedures that are geared only to those children who have disclosed fail to recognize the needs of the majority of victims. **Source: Sorensen & Snow, 1991.**

Study of 630 cases of alleged sexual abuse of children from 1985 through 1989: Using a subset of 116 confirmed cases, findings indicated that 79 percent of the children of the study initially denied abuse or were tentative in disclosing. Of those who did disclose, approximately three-quarters disclosed accidentally. **Source: Sorensen & Snow, 1991.**

Young victims may not recognize their victimization as sexual abuse. **Source: Gilbert, 1988.**

There is the clinical assumption that children who feel compelled to keep sexual abuse a secret suffer greater psychic distress than victims who disclose the secret and receive assistance and support. **Source: Finkelhor & Browne, 1986.**

Early identification of sexual abuse victims appears to be crucial to the reduction of suffering of abused youth and to the establishment of support systems for assistance in pursuing appropriate psychological development and healthier adult functioning. As long as disclosure continues to be a problem for young victims, then fear, suffering, and psychological distress will, like the secret, remain with the victim. **Sources: Bagley, 1992; Bagley, 1991; Finkelhor et al. 1990; Whitlock & Gillman, 1989.**

This documentation taken from: http://www.prevent-abuse-now.com/stats.htm.

ENDNOTES

INTRODUCTION

1. Ritual abuse is organized sexual, physical, and psychological abuse involving rituals, which may or may not be religious in nature.

CHAPTER 1

1. Munchausen (MOON-chou-zun) syndrome is a serious mental disorder in which someone with a deep need for attention pretends to be sick or gets sick or injured on purpose. People with Munchausen syndrome may make up symptoms, push for risky operations, or try to rig laboratory test results in their effort to win sympathy and concern.

Munchausen syndrome belongs to a group of conditions, called factitious disorders, that are either made up or self-inflicted. Factitious disorders can be psychological or physical. Munchausen syndrome refers to the most severe and chronic physical form of factitious disorder. Source: Mayo Clinic (http://www.mayoclinic.com/health/munchausen-syndrome/DS00965)

Photo and Illustration Credits

Publisher's Note: The photographs on both the cover and throughout this book are taken from stock photos and used for illustrative purposes only. It is not to be implied that any of these persons are the victims of abuse.

Cover Photo: "Cathy from B.C. Canada"; used with permission.

Grunge Frame on pages 12, 39, 51, 67, 70, 76, 83, 92, 96: From bigstockphoto.com, Genevieve Rivet; used with permission.

Page 16: From bigstockphoto.com, Sascha Burkard; used with permission; "Skater Kids."

Page 24: From bigstockphoto.com, bratan; used with permission; "empty swing."

Page 30: From bigstockphoto.com; used with permission.

Page 33: From bigstockphoto.com; used with permission.

Page 34: From bigstockphoto.com; Kara Taylor; used with permission, "Boys Walking Black And White."

Page 40: From bigstockphoto.com, ArtPixz; used with permission; "1930 photo of a family."

Page 42: From bigstockphoto.com; used with permission.

Page 44: From bigstockphoto.com; used with permission.

Page 50: From 123rf.com; used with permission; "Portrait of boy."

Page 52: From bigstockphoto.com; used with permission.

Page 58: From istockphoto.com, used with permission.

Page 62: From bigstockphoto.com, ArtPixz; used with permission; "vintage 1943 photo."

Page 64: From bigstockphoto; Joshua Rainey; used with permission; "Three Boys Overlook Canyon."

Page 68: From 123rf.com; Rui Vale De Sousa ; used with permission; "Sad Boy Portrait."

Page 73: From 123rf.com; Elena Ray; used with permission; "Vintage Friends, 1910."

Page 74: From 123rf.com; Nicholas Sutcliffe; used with permission; "Moody teenager with a green hood."

Page 79: From bigstockphoto.com; mandy godbehear; used with permission; "Sad loney child grieving alone."

Page 80: From bigstockphoto.com; ArtPixz; used with permission; "Vintage Family Photo 1938."

Page 86: From 123rf.com; Leah-Anne Thompson; used with permission; "Dejected Boy."

Page 90: From 123rf.com; Noam Armonn; used with permission; "Little Boy Watching the Rain Through the Window."

Page 94: From 123rf.com; Cathy Yeulet; used with permission; "Young boy running on path outdoors smiling."

aBOUT THe aUTHOr

Gregory R Reid, DD, founder of Occult Research & Crime Consultants, has conducted more than 250 training classes for criminal justice workers, police officers, probation departments, and other professionals since 1987. He has spoken extensively in churches nationwide on the dangers of occultism. Gregory has been in youth ministry since 1975 and has worked with at-risk youth, including sexual abuse victims and occult-bound kids. He is an ordained minister, has an honorary doctorate from Logos Graduate School, and has authored eleven books.

Exposing The Darkness Seminar

Never before has the church been in more need of balanced biblical and practical education and preparation to deal with the flood of occultism that has infected this generation.

After many years of preparation and research, Dr. Reid has developed a three-part seminar for this purpose. Designed for both adults and teens, these educational training sessions cover a wide variety of topics, from lures of the occult to dealing with the demonic, from true spiritual warfare to scriptural tools and understanding of that warfare.

These seminars are non-sensational, factual, and completely Bible-based. In twenty-seven years of ministry, Dr. Reid has seen a number of sensationalistic, non-factual, fear-based and conspiracy-oriented workshops under the title "Spiritual warfare" and felt it was crucial to provide a godly, constructive atmosphere and presentation in which believers could learn fact from fantasy, and be equipped with the Word of God to do battle with legitimate works of the enemy.

Part one deals with occult lures, history of idolatry and occultism, and its present effects on our culture and our children.

Part two outlines our Scriptural stand regarding occultic, pagan, and satanic practices, as well as practical guidelines for both leading people to Jesus Christ out of those bondages and setting them free once they become believers.

The third and final dynamic of this seminar is a youth night, geared toward unbelieving kids as well as Christian kids. Dr. Reid presents his testimony of a childhood and adolescence spent in the dark world of real black magick,* both as a victim and later as a practiced, obsessed occultist—with a powerful proclamation of his salvation and deliverance by the power of

---

*This spelling of the word magic usually indicates the more occultic type rather than a performance type, stage magic.

God through meeting Jesus face to face. This evening youth outreach presents a perfect opportunity to bring unsaved kids to Jesus.

These seminar-outreaches have served to equip many believers for frontline warfare against the spirit of this age.

For information on how your church can sponsor the Exposing the Darkness outreach, please contact Gregory Reid at:

YouthFire
Box 370006 El Paso TX 79937
greid@elp.rr.com

References available upon request.

also by Gregory reid

Nobody's Angel

Nobody's Angel is the true story of former occult practitioner Gregory Reid. Born in Southern California, his childhood was a schizophrenic double life of wonderful, loving parents at home- and horrible satanic and sexual abuse outside of their care.

Obsessed with the occult, victimized by pedophiles and on his way to crossing over to black magick, at the age of fifteen he was pursued by Jesus through persistent encounters with Christians until one July night he ended up at a prayer meeting and surrendered his life to Jesus Christ. It was the beginning of new life, an end to the old, and the beginning of a decades-long search for answers to his tormented childhood.

Nobody's Angel is honest, heartbreaking and healing. It is not sensationalistic nor does it glorify the devil, but rather is a powerful testimony of the power of God to deliver and heal even the most shattered of lives. *Nobody's Angel* has helped hundreds of people—especially teens—to understand both the struggle of those who have been wounded and abused and the depth of God's love for every hurting heart. Available through Xulon Press and other online book outlets. Retail: $11.99

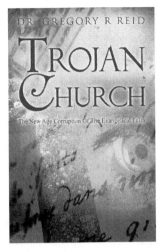

Trojan Church: The New Age Corruption of The Evangelical Faith

We Have Been Invaded. The modern evangelical church is even now undergoing a transformation that is changing its heart and soul and foundation completely. The Future Church is the deliberately designed dream of those moving the world toward globalism, "One World – One Religion." Two or three decades ago, the obstacles to such a transformation were so many as to make the task almost impossible. But, said the tortoise to the hare, slow and steady wins the race. And while the church has run hare-like into trends, megachurch programs and media-driven movements, the New Age tortoise has come into the back door and planted within our walls the tares of deception and illusion that are transforming the church into a New Age Globalist apparatus and puppet from within. Be aware. Be prepared. The Trojan Church is here. Available through Xulon Press and other online book outlets. Retail: $15.99

related resources from Lighthouse Trails

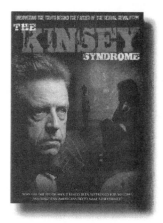

The Kinsey Syndrome
2.5 hour DVD, $19.95

This powerful and sobering film (produced by Christian Pinto and Joe Schimmel) exposes the truth about the sexual revolution that stemmed largely from the work of a man named Dr. Alfred Kinsey, considered by many to be the main influence on today's views of homosexuality, pedophilia, and other sexually deviant behaviors.

The Kinsey Syndrome unfolds the work and influence of Dr. Alfred Kinsey, considered to be "the father of the sexual revolution." But did Kinsey liberate America from its prudish view of sex? Or help to unleash the horrors of our present society?

Laughter Calls Me
by Catherine Brown

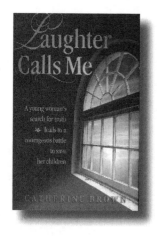

The true story of a young woman who discovers her children have become victims of child pornography. An edge of your seat, hard-to-put-down book. From a hitchhiking hippie of the seventies to a young Christian mom who must flee the country and go into hiding to protect her children, you will embark with her on a most unforgettable journey. This special 2nd edition has family photos and drawings. Retail $12.95, 160 pages with photos.

seDuCers aMONG OUr CHILDreN
by Retired Police Investigator, Patrick Crough

The purpose of this book is to teach all parents and caregivers how to hone their God-given instincts into an effective, knowledge-based tool to protect their children from the child predators who live among us.

This book represents Patrick Crough's personal perspective and is intended to offer a practical, simple presentation of how child predators operate in today's society. It will educate concerned parents and guardians how to recognize when a child predator is in their midst, how to protect their children from predators, how to recognize if a child has already been offended by a predator, and what to do if a child discloses he or she has been offended by a predator. For the adult reader who was sexually molested as a child, this resource may assist you in making some sense out of what happened to you and help you understand it wasn't your fault. Retail $14.95, 272 pages

Lighthouse Trails Publishing Books, CDs & DVDs

BOOKS

Another Jesus (2nd Edition)
by Roger Oakland; $12.95

A Time of Departing, (2nd Ed.)
by Ray Yungen; $12.95

Castles in the Sand
by Carolyn A. Greene, $12.95

Faith Undone
by Roger Oakland, $12.95

For Many Shall Come in My Name
(2nd Edition)
by Ray Yungen; $12.95

Foxe's Book of Martyrs
by John Foxe; $14.95

In My Father's House
by Corrie ten Boom; $13.95

Laughter Calls Me
by Catherine Brown; $12.95

Let There Be Light
by Roger Oakland, $13.95

Muddy Waters
by Nanci Des Gerlaise, $13.95

Stolen from My Arms
by Katherine Sapienza with
Zach Taylor; $14.95

*Stories from Indian Wigwams
and Northern Campfires*
by Egerton Ryerson Young;
$15.95

Strength for Tough Times
by Maria Kneas; $7.95

The Color of Pain
by Gregory Reid; $10.95

The Other Side of the River
by Kevin Reeves, $12.95

Things We Couldn't Say
1st Lighthouse Trails Edition
by Diet Eman; $14.95

Trapped in Hitler's Hell
by Anita Dittman with Jan
Markell; $12.95

DVDs & CDs

The Story of Anita Dittman
with Anita Dittman
$15.95, 60 minutes

The New Face of Mystical Spirituality with Ray Yungen
3 DVD lecture series
$14.95 each or $39.95 for set

Good News in the Badlands
Music CD by Bob Ayanian;
$16.95

To order additional copies of:

THE COLOR OF PAIN

Send $10.95 per book plus shipping to:

Lighthouse Trails Publishing
P.O. Box 908
Eureka, MT 59917
For shipping costs, go to
www.lighthousetrails.com/shippingcosts.htm
($3.95/1-2 books; $5.25/3-5 books; $10.20/5-30 books)

You may also purchase Lighthouse Trails books from
www.lighthousetrails.com.

For bulk (wholesale) rates of 10 or more copies, contact Lighthouse
Trails Publishing, either by phone, online, e-mail, or fax. You may
also order retail or wholesale online at www.lighthousetrails.com,
or for US orders, call our toll-free number:
866/876-3910

For international and all other calls: 406/889-3610
Fax: 406/889-3633

The Color of Pain, as well as other books by Lighthouse Trails
Publishing, can be ordered through all major outlet stores,
bookstores, online bookstores, and Christian bookstores in the
U.S. Bookstores may order through: Ingram, SpringArbor or directly
through Lighthouse Trails.

Libraries may order through Baker & Taylor.

You may visit the author's website at: www.youthfire.com.
You may write to him at:

Gregory Reid
YouthFire Publications
Box 370006 El Paso TX 79937